Is it heavy or light?

Susan Hughes

Crabtree Publishing Company

www.crabtreebooks.com

What's the Matter?

Author: Susan Hughes
Publishing plan research and development:
   Sean Charlebois, Reagan Miller
   Crabtree Publishing Company
Project development: Clarity Content Services
Project management: Karen Iversen
Project coordinator: Kathy Middleton
Editors: Sheila Fletcher, Kathy Middleton
Copy editor: Dimitra Chronopoulos
Proofreader: Reagan Miller
Design: First Image
Photo research: Linda Tanaka
Production coordinator: Margaret Amy Salter
Prepress technician: Margaret Amy Salter
Print coordinator: Katherine Berti

Photographs:
p1 Setaphong Tantanawat/shutterstock; p4-5 mexrix/shutterstock; p5 iStockphoto/Thinkstock; p6 Gelpi/shutterstock; p7 iStockphoto/Thinkstock; p8 left Geoffrey Holman/iStock, Christian Delbert/shutterstock; p9 left Ingvar Bjork/shutterstock, Hemera/Thinkstock; p10 left Sergii Figurnyi/shutterstock, Johan Swanepoel/shutterstock; p11 top right Bob Orsillo/shutterstock, Gelpi/shutterstock; p12 iStockphoto/Thinkstock; p13 Nataliya Hora/shutterstock; p14 iStockphoto/Thinkstock; p15 PhotoObjects.net/Thinkstock; p16 ben bryant/shutterstock; p17 Bergamont/shutterstock, ben Bryant/shutterstock; p19 left valdis torms/shutterstock, Mikael Goransson/shutterstock; p20 Reincarnation/shutterstock; p21 iStockphoto/Thinkstock; p22 top gracious_tiger/shutterstock, Losevsky Pavel/shutterstock, iStockphoto/Thinkstock; cover shutterstock

Library and Archives Canada Cataloguing in Publication

Hughes, Susan, 1960-
   Is it heavy or light? / Susan Hughes.

(What's the matter?)
Includes index.
Issued also in electronic formats.
ISBN 978-0-7787-2048-5 (bound).--ISBN 978-0-7787-2055-3 (pbk.)

   1. Weight (Physics)--Juvenile literature. 2. Matter--Properties--Juvenile literature. I. Title. II. Series: What's the matter? (St. Catharines, Ont.)

QC106.H84 2012   j620.1'129   C2012-900291-7

Library of Congress Cataloging-in-Publication Data

Hughes, Susan, 1960-
Is it heavy or light? / Susan Hughes.
p. cm. -- (What's the matter?)
Includes index.
ISBN 978-0-7787-2048-5 (reinforced library binding : alk. paper) -- ISBN 978-0-7787-2055-3 (pbk. : alk. paper) -- ISBN 978-1-4271-7946-3 (electronic pdf) -- ISBN 978-1-4271-8061-2 (electronic html)
1. Weight (Physics)--Juvenile literature. 2. Matter--Properties--Juvenile literature. I. Title.

QC106.H84 2012
531'.5--dc23
           2012000118

Crabtree Publishing Company

www.crabtreebooks.com   1-800-387-7650

Printed in the U.S.A./032012/CJ20120215

Published in Canada
Crabtree Publishing
616 Welland Ave.
St. Catharines, ON
L2M 5V6

Published in the United States
Crabtree Publishing
PMB 59051
350 Fifth Avenue, 59th Floor
New York, New York 10118

Published in the United Kingdom
Crabtree Publishing
Maritime House
Basin Road North, Hove
BN41 1WR

Published in Australia
Crabtree Publishing
3 Charles Street
Coburg North
VIC 3058

What is in this book?

What is matter?

How are a light feather and a heavy rock the same?

They are both made of **matter**.

Matter is anything that takes up space and has **mass**.

Mass is the amount of material in an object.

Everything you can see, feel, touch, and taste is matter.

You are made of matter, too!

What is a property?

Matter has **properties**.

Properties describe how something looks, feels, tastes, smells, or sounds.

We can look at an object to learn about its color and shape.

Color and shape are properties.

We can lift an
object to learn if
it is heavy or light.

The words heavy and
light describe **weight**.

Weight is a property, too.

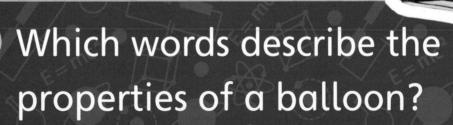

? Which words describe the
properties of a balloon?
- heavy
- round
- rough
- light
- square
- smooth

Some materials are **heavy**.

They weigh a lot.

This bulldozer is heavy.
It is used to push heavy
piles of dirt.

This wrecking ball is heavy.

It is used to knock down
big buildings.

8

Some materials are **light**.

They do not weigh very much.

A coin is light so you
can carry it in your pocket.

A hair clip is light so it
will not be too heavy
for your head.

? What does a boat anchor
do? Does an anchor need
to be heavy or light?

Big or small

Often, a big object is heavy, and a small object is light.

An elephant is big and heavy.

 A goldfish is small and light.

But look!

A hot air balloon is big, but it is light.

A hand weight is small, but it is heavy.

Sometimes big objects are light.

Sometimes small objects are heavy.

What else is big and light?

What else is small and heavy?

What is it made of?

One way to tell if an object is heavy or light is to find out what materials it is made of.

Bubble Wrap is made out of plastic. The bubbles are filled with air. The plastic and air are light.

Bubble Wrap is light.

A car has many steel parts.

Steel is heavy. A car is heavy, too.

Use a scale

We can weigh things using a **scale**.

A scale is a tool used to measure weight.

It tells us how heavy or light things are.

Put an object on a scale.

The arrow points at a number.

The number tells how much the object weighs.

Which weighs more, the apple or the melon?

Brain teaser: Which is heavier—one pound (453 grams) of feathers or one pound (453 grams) of bricks?

Use a balance

We can also measure objects using a **balance**.

A balance is a tool that measures mass. It tells us how much matter is in an object.

A heavy object has more mass than a light object.

The side of a balance that holds an object with the most mass will go down. The side with the object with less mass will go up.

Which has more mass,
the red block or the
paper clip?

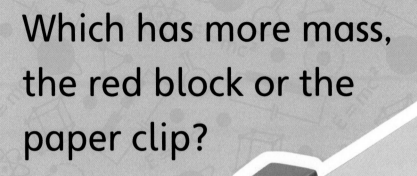

Which is heavier, the green
block or the red checker?

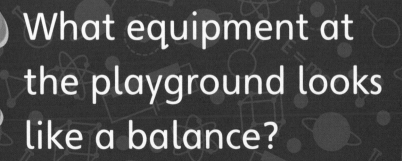

What equipment at
the playground looks
like a balance?

Not heavier, not lighter

Sometimes neither side of the balance goes up or down.

The objects on each side are balanced, or in the same position.

That is because the objects have the same mass.

They weigh the same.

How is a seesaw
like a balance?

How would you make one
side of the seesaw heavier?

Compare weights!

A

Try to guess which object in each picture is heavier and which is lighter.

B

C

C the bowling ball is heavier; the balloon is lighter

B the adult is heavier; the child is lighter

A the adult giraffe is heavier; the baby giraffe is lighter

Words to know and Index

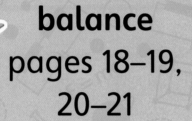

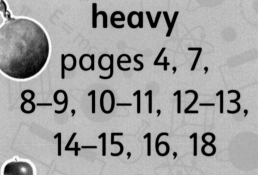

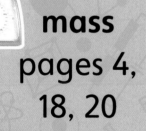

23

Notes for adults

Objectives
- to introduce children to the difference between heavy and light objects
- to learn how people weigh objects
- to compare and describe objects based on their weight

Prerequisite
Ask the children to read *Is it transparent or opaque?* before reading *Is it heavy or light?* Introducing them to the concepts of matter via *Is it transparent or opaque?* will help familiarize them with the initial concepts in this book.

Questions before reading *Is it heavy or light?*
"What things are heavy? What things are light?"

"Tell me about a time you carried something that was heavy."

"How is something that is small different from something that is light?"

"Have you ever been weighed? How were you weighed?"

Discussion
Read the book to the children. Discuss with the children some of the main concepts in the book, such as heavy and light, weight, and scales.

Have the children close their eyes. Place objects in their hands and ask them to say which is heavy and which is light.

Then encourage the children to use a kitchen scale or a balance. Ask them to compare the weights of the objects based on their observations. Ask if many items are always heavier than fewer items. Ask if smaller objects always weigh less than bigger objects.

Extension
Cut out pictures from magazines or advertisements. Make a graph with the word HEAVY on one side and the word LIGHT on the other side. Have the children sort the pictures. Discuss with them how they made their choices.

What's the Matter?

Is it flexible or rigid?
Is it heavy or light?
Is it hot or cold?
Is it magnetic or nonmagnetic?
Is it smooth or rough?
Is it transparent or opaque?

Guided Reading: K

U.S.A.	$6.95
Canada	$7.95

CRABTREE
Publishing Company
www.crabtreebooks.com

ISBN 978-0-7787-2055-3

9 780778 720553

50695